Wind

Look for the other books on weather by

Marion Dane Bauer
Snow • Rain • Clouds

First Aladdin edition September 2003

Text copyright © 2003 by Marion Dane Bauer
Illustrations copyright © 2003 by John Wallace

ALADDIN PAPERBACKS
An imprint of Simon & Schuster Children's Publishing Division
1230 Avenue of the Americas
New York, NY 10020

Book design by Debra Sfetsios
The text of this book was set in Century Schoolbook.

Printed in the United States of America
2 4 6 8 10 9 7 5 3 1

Library of Congress Cataloging-in-Publication Data

Bauer, Marion Dane.
Wind / Marion Dane Bauer ; illustrated by John Wallace.— 1st Aladdin
Paperbacks ed.
p. cm. — (Ready-to-read)
Summary: Illustrations and simple text explain what wind is, how it is
used by plants, birds, and people, and how wind can become a storm.
ISBN 0-689-85443-9 (pbk.) — ISBN 0-689-85442-0 (library ed.)
1. Winds—Juvenile literature. [1. Winds.] I. Wallace, John, 1966–
ill. II. Title. III. Series.

QC931.4.B38 2004
551.51'8—dc21

2002009656

Wind

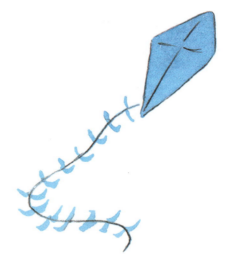

written by Marion Dane Bauer

illustrated by John Wallace

Aladdin

New York London Toronto Sydney Singapore

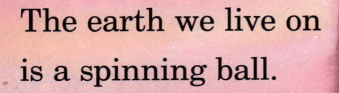

The earth we live on
is a spinning ball.

When the earth spins,
the air around it
moves too.

When air moves,
we call it "wind."
As the sun heats the air,
the air grows lighter.
Light air rises.

Cool air is heavy.

It falls.

Cool air and warm air
are always trading places.

We call this movement "wind."

Birds use wind
to help them fly.

Plants use wind
to carry their seeds.

We use wind
to fly kites,

to sail boats,

and to turn
windmills.

Wind moves clouds.
Wind makes waves.
It even makes trees bend.

When the hot air
is very light
and the cold air
is very heavy,
wind can blow up a storm!

Sometimes wind spins
like a puppy
chasing its tail.

A small spin
makes a dust devil
or a water spout.

A strong spin
makes a tornado
or a hurricane.

Wind can be scary.

Or it can sing
a gentle song.

Wind is all around us,
but we cannot see it.

We can only see
what wind does.

Facts about wind:

The air that surrounds the Earth is called the troposphere. It is only about eight miles deep.

The hardest gust of wind ever measured was on Mount Washington. It was 231 miles per hour.

When wind blows snow very hard, we have a blizzard.

The eye of a hurricane is still. The winds are quiet there. After the eye passes, the winds blow in the opposite direction.